Read for a
Better World™

SHARKS
A First Look

PERCY LEED

GRL Consultants,
Diane Craig and Monica Marx,
Certified Literacy Specialists

Lerner Publications ◆ Minneapolis

TABLE OF CONTENTS

Sharks

Sharks are fish.
They live in oceans
all over the world.

There are many kinds of sharks.

One is longer than a bus.
One is shorter than a
baseball bat.

A shark has fins.
The back fin helps it swim.

The top fin helps it balance.

9

Sharks breathe
underwater
using gills.
Sharks can smell
in water too.

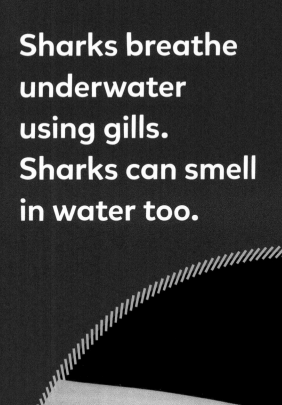

gills

How might smelling
underwater
be useful?

Sharks are darker on top.
This helps them hunt
animals above them.

The sharks blend in with
the water below.

Shark bellies are a light color. This helps them hunt animals below them.

The shark bellies blend in with the water above.

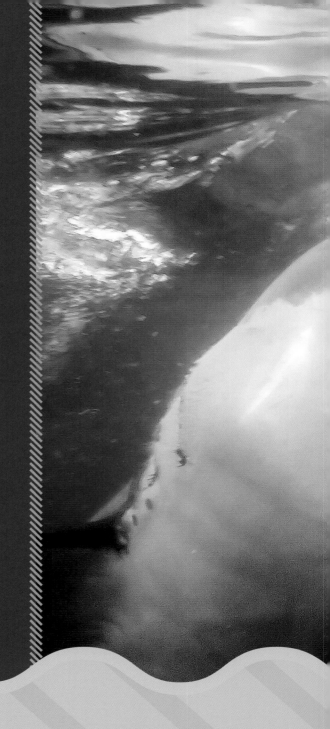

Sharks have rows of sharp teeth. Great white sharks can have 300 teeth!

How do you think sharp teeth help sharks hunt?

A whale shark eats with its mouth open. It catches small animals.

Baby sharks are called pups.
They take care of themselves.

You Connect!

What is something you like about sharks?

Have you ever seen a video of a shark?

What other ocean animals do you know about?

STEM Snapshot

Encourage students to think and ask questions like scientists. Ask the reader:

What is something you learned about sharks?

What is something you noticed about shark bodies?

What is something you still want to learn about sharks?

Photo Glossary

fin

gills

pup

teeth

Learn More

Boyer, Crispin. *So Cool! Sharks*. Washington, DC: National Geographic Kids, 2019.

de la Bédoyère, Camilla. *Swim! Shark!* Mankato, MN: QEB Publishing, 2021.

McGuire, David. *Sharks for Kids: A Junior Scientist's Guide to Great Whites, Hammerheads, and Other Sharks in the Sea*. Emeryville, CA: Rockridge Press, 2020.

Index

Photo Acknowledgments

The images in this book are used with the permission of: © Aaronejbull87/Shutterstock Images, pp. 20, 23 (pup); © atese/iStockphoto, p. 12; © fotosparrow/Shutterstock Images, p. 15; © J nel/Shutterstock Images, p. 13; © kaschibo/Shutterstock Images, p. 6; © Martin Voeller/Shutterstock Images, p. 8; © Michael Geyer/iStockphoto, pp. 9, 23 (fin); © Nicolas Sanchez-Biezma/iStockphoto, p. 14; © pjohnson1/iStockphoto, pp. 10, 23 (gills); © Richard Condlyffe/Shutterstock Images, pp. 10–11; © richcarey/iStockphoto, pp. 18–19; © Serge Melesan/iStockphoto, pp. 4–5; © Vincent Legrand/Shutterstock Images, pp. 16–17, 23 (teeth); © Vladimir Wrangel/Shutterstock Images, p. 7.

Cover Photo: © VisionDive/Shutterstock Images

Design Elements: © Mighty Media, Inc.

Lerner Publications Company
An imprint of Lerner Publishing Group, Inc.
241 First Avenue North
Minneapolis, MN 55401 USA

For reading levels and more information, look up this title at www.lernerbooks.com.

Main body text set in Mikado a Medium.
Typeface provided by Hannes von Doehren.

Library of Congress Cataloging-in-Publication Data

Names: Leed, Percy, 1968- author.
Title: Sharks : a first look / Percy Leed.
Description: Minneapolis : Lerner Publications, [2023] | Series: Read about ocean animals (read for a better world) | Includes bibliographical references and index. | Audience: Ages 5-8 | Audience: Grades K–1 | Summary: "Sharks are the most famous hunters of the sea. Simple text and engaging photos introduce readers to these awesome ocean animals"— Provided by publisher.
Identifiers: LCCN 2021051181 (print) | LCCN 2021051182 (ebook) | ISBN 9781728459141 (library binding) | ISBN 9781728464183 (paperback) | ISBN 9781728461731 (ebook)
Subjects: LCSH: Sharks—Juvenile literature.
Classification: LCC QL638.9 .L43 2023 (print) | LCC QL638.9 (ebook) | DDC 597.3—dc23/eng/20211022

LC record available at https://lccn.loc.gov/2021051181
LC ebook record available at https://lccn.loc.gov/2021051182

Manufactured in the United States of America
1 – CG – 7/15/22